how to stay afloat:
the art of drowning

poems by

samantha "sammy" herrera

how to stay afloat
© 2025 Samantha Herrera
ISBN: 978-1-966337-22-5
First Edition, 2025

Printed in the United States of America

Edited by: Hannah Astrid Noble
Cover Design by: Luis Martinez
Layout Design by: Erica Castro

For my parents
Who have fine pressed me into who I am

For Henry
Who showed me love in the purest form, unconditionally and
unapologetically.
I love you forever, honey

For myself
In all of the broken, you have always come out as who you are
meant to be: light, love, and poetry

Sammy's words are strong like the bridge city of La Puente. Her poems move like shadows, sparring with silence and breaking down walls of complacency. Rooted in community and family, her verses dance across the page with grit and grace, speaking truths that refuse to stay quiet. She doesn't just slam poems—she slams love, memory, and everything we're told to keep inside.
Ceasar K. Avelar (2nd poet Laureate of Pomona), author of *God of the Air Hose*

How to stay afloat: the art of drowning, despite its title, is an absolute breath of fresh air. Samantha "Sammy" Herrera's debut collection is utterly unique and unafraid to challenge conceptions of love, culture, sexism, and society. Her work explores these themes in profound ways, submerging you in beautiful metaphors and powerful messages that pull you deeper into the pages, thirsting for more. Sammy's poetry washes over you in both gentle tides and the crushing force of a wave.
Peter Lechuga, author of *Myth Opportunities*

Samantha Herrera is a generational poet with a sharp tongue that slices through the noise, cutting straight to the truth. Yet, within that sharpness lies an undeniable tenderness—an invitation into the intricacies of a wounded heart, one that aches, heals, and keeps beating. *how to stay afloat: the art of drowning* is a force, pulling readers into experiences only Herrera can render with such vividness, rawness, and beauty. Each poem lands like a punch to the gut, shaping vignettes of a life entirely her own—yet deeply familiar to us all. Through striking imagery and masterful nuance, she crafts a world where every word carries weight, where nothing is wasted. This is a book for the children of immigrants, the heartbroken and the heartbreakers, the policymakers, the haters, the lovers, and the homies. Herrera gives voice to the voiceless—and what a voice it is.
Alexis Jaimes, author of *Corazón Coalesced*

Samantha Herrera's collection *how to stay afloat: the art of drowning* enters each poem with "a Barbie smile and grin" as she fearlessly calls out, confronts and questions the various cruelties of the world around her, both past and present. As Herrera recognizes the aftermath of these violences, the speaker still chooses to move forward, take control and find joy in the little moments. Moments as simple as, "I made pancakes in the morning/ And found myself crying/I will enjoy my breakfast/Dry up any leftover tears/ And place my memories in a to go box for another day."
Karla Cordero, Author of *How To Pull Apart The Earth*

In *how to stay afloat: the art of drowning*, Samantha Herrera offers readers a piercing, intimate portrait of a life shaped by forces much larger than the self. Through her vivid poems, she shows how love, loss, violence, culture, memory, and language are not isolated experiences, but deeply intertwined with the world we move through — how the personal and political are never truly separate.

Herrera's work refuses to flatten human experience into simple stories. Her poems on love, such as "muse" and "isn't this where you met the sun?", capture not just the joy and heartbreak of relationships, but how even private emotions are entangled with memory, art, and the drive to create meaning beyond ourselves. Love, for Herrera, is an act that connects past, present, and future — a reminder that our emotions are always in dialogue with the stories we inherit and the dreams we imagine.

When she addresses trauma, Herrera confronts the ways violence is woven into everyday life. In "boys will be boys" and "hands on fire," she illuminates how cultural excuses and gendered expectations allow harm to fester, how bodies and memories carry the marks of a society that too often looks away. These are not simply poems of individual suffering; they are testimonies about what it means to live in a world where harm is normalized and survival becomes an act of quiet rebellion.

Identity and belonging are also central concerns. In "my american tongue," Herrera explores the disorienting experience of feeling severed from ancestral roots — not by choice, but by the pressures of assimilation, language loss, and cultural displacement. She captures the ache of navigating multiple worlds, never fully at home in either, and the quiet grief of realizing that names, languages, and traditions are not just personal markers but shared inheritances that can be both bridges and battlegrounds.

Throughout *how to stay afloat: the art of drowning*, Herrera reveals how deeply individuals are shaped by the worlds they inhabit — whether that world is a classroom rehearsing lockdown drills ("not a place for guns"), a culture that fails to protect its most vulnerable ("Blessed are the homies"), or a society that diminishes racism into "microaggressions" disguised as jokes. These poems lay bare how external realities etch themselves into internal landscapes, leaving scars, but also forging unexpected sources of strength.

And yet, Herrera's work is not simply a chronicle of hurt. It is equally a testament to resilience, tenderness, and the stubborn persistence of hope. Even when love dissolves, even when belonging feels fractured, even when violence looms large, her poems find ways to rebuild from ruins — to honor what has been lost and to imagine what might yet be possible.

Herrera's mastery of language — her ability to stitch together vivid imagery, biting critique, and raw emotion — makes each poem feel like both a private confession and a public witnessing. Her writing reminds us that we are not islands, but shaped by the rivers that run through us: history, culture, community, violence, hope.

How to stay afloat: the art of drowning is a powerful meditation on how the world marks us, challenges us, and sometimes, despite everything, teaches us to bloom. Samantha Herrera's voice is one that deserves to be heard — clear, urgent, and unafraid to tell the complicated truths of what it means to be alive.

This is a book for anyone who has felt the weight of the world inside their own skin — and for anyone who still believes that even the most broken ground can yield something beautiful.

In Short:
In *how to stay afloat: the art of drowning*, Samantha Herrera traces the deep ways that love, loss, violence, and identity are shaped by the worlds we inhabit. Her poems reveal how personal experiences are entangled with cultural expectations, language, memory, and survival. Through vivid storytelling and powerful imagery, Herrera captures how the forces around us leave their imprint on our bodies, dreams, and relationships — and how, even from fractured ground, resilience can take root. This is a collection about how we are made and remade by the world — and how we find ways to speak, remember, and rebuild.
Prof. Ant Black aka Dr. Anthony Blacksher

"In Samantha's collection, *how to stay afloat: the art of drowning* - Samantha weaves a deeply emotional narrative that drives the reader instantly. Each poem is beautifully written. I could not stop reading them. Her words are powerful and I can already imagine these poems being performed at an open mic. Samantha's voice leads us through moments of pain, joy, and reflection, ultimately inviting readers to embark on their own personal exploration. *how to stay afloat: the art of drowning* -is a must-read for any reader!" Celeste Alyssa Gomez, Author & Founder of La Poeta Publications.

Acknowledgments

To all that have supported me and my art- thank you for seeing potential in me, for pushing me forward into the uncomfortable and the unknown, for supporting me, and enjoying this journey with me. I wouldn't have made it this far without the community, my people, my village. I am grateful in every universe.

Henry- thank you for being my muse. I love you.

My parents & my brother—thank you for being by my side. Thank you for letting me be a mess and loving me through it all. You are everything.

Cory Besskepp Cofer & A Mic & Dim Lights— I'm not sure if there would be poetry in my life if it wasn't for you. Thank you for reminding me of my roots; it all started in f-5 at a little high school in La Puente. It was because of you that I published my first poem and found my voice at open mics. Thank you for giving me a start and watching me grow as a poet. I hope I continue making you proud. I can't wait for more embarrassing "proud dad" introductions at open mics.

Ceasar K. Avelar—from day one, you saw a spark in me and regifted me a home in poetry at Obsidian Tongues open mic. Thank you for seeing the grit in me and giving me a space to embrace the rugged poet in me. Just like Bess, I hope to grace more stages with you where you can give an embarrassing "proud dad" introduction.

Luis- I cannot begin to thank you enough for being part of this process. I've loved your art since I've met you and having your work as a part of my very first book means everything. I can't wait for my words and your art to travel around the world together.

Patrick- your friendship has truly helped me heal. I am so thankful for all the bestie dates, good laughs, and crying. I hope you understand how grateful I am for you. Thank you for supporting my poetry and being such a good friend to me.

My TA, Consuelo- thank you for making me a better poet and writer. Your feedback has helped me grow in ways I didn't know I needed. Thank you for loving my art and reminding me to use my voice.

David A. Romero—the day you visited my high school for a poetry workshop has continued to impact me as a writer and spoken word artist in more ways than one. "My Name is Romero" is my favorite poem and book of yours to this day. Thank you for inspiring me through the years. I am grateful that I am lucky enough to share stages with you.

Prof. Anthony Black—you have seen me since I was a baby poet just starting out and have always believed in me. I am glad you are witnessing my comeback into poetry. I have nothing but gratitude for your wisdom and faith in me and my poetry. Thank you.

Rudy Francisco- I swear to god, your poetry has altered my brain chemistry. Thank you for your talent and for being a constant inspiration. Thank you for your words and the way they remind me that being alive is worth it all.

Dr. M, my sweet therapist—thank you for always being proud of me. Thank you for being gentle with me and believing I could do the hard things, when I didn't think I could. You have helped me make it out of the hardest times and continue to help me learn, navigate, and grow. I am so thankful for you.

My lovely poet friends—each of you are exactly what I needed in this journey of poetry and finishing this book. I am grateful for your feedback and support in everything my messy brain has created.

My poet bestie— Peter Lechuga— thank you for being such a foundation. I appreciate everything you've done for me, from workshopping pieces to hyping me up on stage. I am grateful for our friendship. I'm also so grateful for meeting Jannette through you.

Lopez Urban Farm—the farm is easily one of my favorite places in Pomona and is turning into a second home for me. Thank you, Farmer Stephen, for opening your doors not only for myself and other poets, but to the community.

To the City of Pomona—who I believe is magic, thank you for pulling me back to where poetry started for me and where it now continues to thrive.

Table of Contents

Nogales High School rests 20 minutes east of Los Angeles in La Puente CA. About 45 minutes from the beach and mountains, the city once known for its citrus and avocados is also known for its nostalgic Old Town on Main street and its iconic often photographed Donut Holes infrastructure. La Puente is also a working class city and has had its share of gang activity and violence.

The latter could be why a school like Nogales, full of ambitious, motivated teens, was once surrounded by black iron bars. As an educator and advisor of the Nogales Poetry Club, I was intentional in providing a safe space for students to write and express themselves through poetry. On the other side of those black bars was a group of students who were part of a club that felt connected by sharing experiences and inspiring empathy. They were proudly the 'student voice' of the campus, and soon began to take field trips to nearby schools to conduct student-led poetry workshops.

Sammy, a sophomore and aspiring journalist at the time, asked to roll along to write about our upcoming poetry workshop. Inspired, she joined the club and as a senior, became our club president while blossoming as a leader and a writer.

After attending the University of La Verne and becoming an educator, Samantha has become a fixture in the greater Los Angeles poetry community. Her debut collection of poems, *how to stay afloat: the art of drowning* is filled with richly layered images and precise language.

Every moment is a passage of time and what changes it brings— "I like to live where I no longer belong/it somehow makes me feel whole again." Herrerra's subtle use of humor allows her to address the difficult emotions associated with adulthood and the complex relationships experienced— "Dust collected folk tales/Waiting for anyone to listen to the stories of our happy/The same reason vinegar and baking soda cannot hold hands/We react too vividly/Fall apart too easily"

how to stay afloat: the art of drowning reminds us of the beauty that surrounds us and the black iron bars we look past. It reminds us how life can be as simple as avocados mixed with a little citrus. These poems speak of nostalgia, lessons learned and a life examined through the eyes of a talented poet who initially chose to test the waters after riding along on a field trip. Now, she is—drowning in poetry.

Preface

When I was teaching second grade, one of my students asked me what I would do if I wasn't a teacher. I told her I would write a book, to which her response was, "why not do both?" I don't know why the answer was so simple or why I never thought of doing both or what I was waiting for, better timing? Better poems? More time? I don't know. That year of teaching was probably the worst year of my life—I was dealing with so much loss, and I didn't know how to cope. I didn't know if I was going to make it to the next day.

I used to write poetry all the time—it was such a huge part of who I was and for maybe 5 (or more?) years I let it go, put it on the back burner, and let myself get lost in the bright lights, the crowds, and someone else's stage. I think love really is that blinding. But when you lose it—when it leaves you, you're forced to find your footing—you're forced to be ok and get better.

This is not an invite to a pity party—shit happens, people change, people fall out of love, people stay in love, people grow apart, people aren't who you thought they would be, your life's plan falls apart and you're derailed. It all really, really sucks.

But, I think I needed this. I needed it all to slip though my fingers for this book to finally happen. For me to choose myself.

Originally, this book had a different title—something about sunflowers. When I finally got to the book cover process, the title and art concepts didn't sit well with me. It kept me up at night. It took me a long time to realize that this first title was still paying homage to who I lost—to who left me with no regrets, no remorse, no more loving eyes. But who am I to speak for them? To assume their feelings through my own pain and heartache? Perhaps there was regret, sympathy, remorse. Maybe they did love me still and this was their way of showing me they loved themselves too. Maybe I thought they'd read it and know that I'm doing better, I'm alive, I'm moving forward, I'm not this ugly depressed, controlling, irrational being they saw me as. Maybe they'd see how much progress I've made. Maybe they'd see that I miss them, and they'd realize they miss me too. Maybe this would change the distance between us. Maybe if this book title was for them, things would work out better this time. But the reality settled and here I am.

I've cried.
I've mourned.
I still mourn.
For them. For us. For me.

I changed the title to what felt right. If I didn't find my way back into poetry, if I didn't find this community, if I didn't invest in something I love—something I am good at—something that's for myself, I don't think I would have made it to where I am now. I was drowning myself in poetry—writing it, reading it, going to open mics, going to workshops, and making poet friends. Drowning in all of this poetry was the only thing that kept me afloat.

This book mourns with me. It mourns who I lost, it mourns who I loved, it mourns so many versions of myself—it mourns but it moves on, and I am trying to do the same.

I hope this book does what it needs to do. I hope it speaks for itself. I hope it helps others in their healing. I hope it inspires people. I hope it stays a reminder for myself that I have made it out alive.

how to stay afloat:
the art of drowning

rivers, oceans,
lakes, and puddles
for you

```
        falling in love
        (the first poem I ever wrote you)
```

When I was little
I wanted to grow up to be a singer
In the third grade
Before I signed up for the talent show
My mom told me I couldn't sing
That was the last time I sang

>So why is it that I find myself
>>singing for you
>Practicing melodies
>Memorizing lyrics
>Figuring out harmonies

>You remind me of a dream
>You remind me of a song
>You remind me
>of the reason
>>I wanted to sing in the first place

loving you is easy

I love you in all seasons
In the sweaty summer
Sticky kisses
Clammy hands
Clasped
Collecting some of my favorite memories
Storing them in time capsules
For the next solstice

      I love you
      In California winters
      Below 70 degrees
      Your warmth keeps me grounded
      Reminiscent of the earth
      Core to mantle
      Bringing me back to the beginning of time
      When the ice was all the world knew
      I've known you in all my past lives
      Through the rain and storms
      You the thunder
      Me the lighting
      Finding my way back to you
      Every time
      Always

I love you
In the spring
We grow like dandelions
Spreading fast
And far
A wishful dream
Eyes are closed
A smile decorated in a hopeful haze
Inhale small
And blow
And dream
And I wish for you
Every chance I get

I love you
In the fall
Falling fast
For you
Your smile
Your way of bringing light into all places you exist
I want to step on every crunchy leaf with you
Hold you as trees change colors
Green
Orange
Brown
Gliding to the floor
A dance of nature
Waiting for the days to become shorter
The nights longer

In all seasons
I love you
Through your changes
Shifting into a new soul tied to the same shadow
Reborn
Again and again
Never retracing old steps
I admire you
For never staying the same
Not a stagnant bone in your body
You have always been a dreamer
That I want to keep up with

music for lovers

I found metronomes in your voice
  And I can't help but follow your tempo
    As you lead me to your body
      A temple
  Let me stay lost in you
    In your wavelengths
      Tangled in your sound
  Reminding me of the way love echoes
    I can hear our movements
      They are an ensemble
        Playing parallel
We sway
  as if we've done this our whole lives
    This
    is how you say

    I love you

      With no noise

        In our silence
I love you

    Radio static

    White noise

      The hum is comforting

  We stay swirling

    In a mess of chords

    and strums

      And pauses

always find me

In crowded rooms

Between shapes and shadows
Figures of familiar
In the architecture of the unknown

I see you flicker and flame
Guide in the warmth

Almost inaudible
I can hear you
Call me in close

In the quietest undertones
You reach for my hand
Hold me in your glances
Tightly

You love me here
In the temporary

Finding me in the forever
Lost in algorithms
You are never far

In the distance
I watch you search for me
Where there are too many people

Static on screens
Busy streets

In the flocks
In the swarms
In the seas
You still look for me

Every single time
You find me

found

I found you

At a place and time
Where love had signed the ends of all my edges
But I found you
With a smile and a kind heart
I fell into you
Deeply
Hopelessly
And forever in love
You had always been familiar
Like a face from a reoccurring dream
I think you've always known me
Searched for me subconsciously
I can already feel the
reincarnation of us
Holding hands in
another universe
Inevitably bound together
Magnetic friction
An endless game of hide and seek
A flutter of memories from every lifetime we've lived
Fill us up
Brings the warm and fuzzy feeling of 'I've been here before'
Begging the question
Of how many lives we have lived
How many times we have met
How many more moments will lead me

back

to

you

lips

There is love on your lips
I can feel it
As you press them on my skin
Slow and soft
There is kindness in the embrace
The goosebumps collectively say
You make me nervous
In the best way
I count every single millisecond
Ticking away
Until the next moment
You are so close to me
That your heartbeat starts to narrate
Falling in love all over again
Like the first time

my name

I still like the way you say my name
    The way the syllables sound
            The cadence
      The inflection of love
Lined up in perfect unison
      Blind folded
         About to be executed by firing squad
      The last inhale
      A silent exhale
      Waiting for death
           Say it again
           Say it again
           Say it again
    My name
    Leaps from your mouth
      Waiting to be followed by I love you
      In the silence
      I hold my breath
         Waiting for your voice to vibrate
           Rattle my heart
               Shake my core
    I hear
      The ringing
You are so melodic as you speak

      My name
        Loves to spill from your mouth
Every
      Single
        Time
          You say
            My name
It is ceremonial
      A celebration of intimacy and tenderness
         Say it again
         Say it again
         Say it again

4/2

You are not just a 2 am late night
Early morning thought
You are love that unwinds my inner clock
I love you at all hours
As we move clockwise by design
Gravity is working in the opposite direction
A pull
I reach for you still
Now our hands only graze each other at the hour
As we move past one another
In a millisecond
I hold you close
Inhale your love
Gone
I miss you
Another roundabout until the next
I count down the next 60 minutes
Until I can grace your presence
Once more
Until
We meet again
I love you at all hours
I love you at all hours
I love you at all hours
I love you

muse

Because I love you
I've turned you into art
Poorly painted memories across awkward canvases
Laughter etched into acrylic
You could almost hear the joy
Half finished sketches
Of your hands
The tips of your fingers
The crevasses of your lifelines
The warmth that you ease into my busy mind
I water color you into an infinity pool of forget-me-nots
Pulled petals glued into notebooks
Pressed into a preserved state
Where we lie head against head in time
Frozen
Snapshot moments
Photographs that plant kisses in my brain
Lightbulbs glow
And I remember everything
But mostly
You

And the poems
The poems
The metaphors that spill from my spirit
Anchor me into a choke hold with cupid
Without any effort
I'd describe you in love
Move mountains into stanzas
Never enough words to define you
On paper
In lost journals hidden in the deepest parts of my arteries
On scraps of paper
Anywhere words could hold value
I write about you
In dreams
And in death
You are every haiku
Limerick
Sonnet
Ballad
Every verse and lyric
All my rhymes and rhymes

I've turned you dancer
Watched you waltz into all of my fantasies
Plié into my streams of consciousness
Sway me into a lullaby trance
Spin and swing
Twist and twirl
I could gaze at you forever
Amazed by every ounce of you
I call you muse
My heart always inspired
You make my dreams have dreams
All because I love you
And turned you into my favorite art

sundays

You remind me of Sundays
Sleepy mornings
Tired eyes
Begging
For more hours
Stay
Just a little longer
It is so easy to fall lost in you
Follow the rivers in your palms
Make blueprints and build homes
Live on daydreams
A safe space on the edge of reality
Before we have to clock into the chaos of everyone else
We can make our bed
Fluff the pillows
And stay rested in the arms of my favorite day

love me in poetry

Burry me in prose
Lose me in unfinished stanzas
In stories I couldn't tell
But only dreamed
In the metaphors I couldn't remember
Lay me with all of the words
That did not make it to see the light of day
Pry my eulogy from the corners of my throat
My flowers
Made from the poems that prayed for me to stay alive
Place the bouquet next to my favorite verse
Let the decay kiss me goodbye
Marry me to the earth
Where forever
Will know me well
My gravestone
Will call me poet
My loved ones
Will call me back to the living
But I will remain here
Where lovers go to write
Where writers go to rest

time, time, time

Time was probably a dancer in another life
          Skipping stones on water top
                    Letting it ripple
          And bend into something new and broken
Something I knew
          And repaired
          My hands have turned hourglass
Still trying to hold you
Still a home of minutes
                    Waiting for you
                    Giving you air to breathe
An arsenal of oxygen
Shaped like space
                    Resembling distance
A reflection of missed moments
And mistakes brushed under a dirty rug
Apologies mapped in constellations

               I love you in sundials
               Checking on the shadows
          Letting them hold me as I wait
               I hear the pendulum
          And it sounds like your voice
               Saying I love you
          A smile creases into my skin
               Without effort
          You make me happy
          You are the light that travel
               From space to my eyes
               A vision of love
          Glowing brighter and stronger
          Expanding parallel to the universe

                    Infinite
                    Not a crossed thought of ever ending
                    I think my heart is a clock
                    Intervals make me into waves of missing you
                    Reminding me
                    You will always be worth the wait

try again

Starting over
Tastes like vanilla
Moves through small spaces

Slowly

And cautiously
But still moves
Forward
Just like us
A new beginning
Find me at square one
At the entrance
Painting the dawn

Hi

My name is a colloquial for fool
Which explains why love paints me a jester
My eyes blink passion
A kiss of charming in every flutter
I get a little anxious
But I am a fighter
Wrestling the pressure my brain tries to drown me in
I wish I could sing
But I am a cracked music note
Trying not to be heard
Looking for a home
Settling in the uncomfortable

I don't know how to dance
But I still try
I love sunflowers
Because they remind me
I have poetry etched into my bones
I am a writer
A lover
A fighter
Sometimes a mistake
My throat closes up with apologies
My tears sometimes overpower me

But I'm learning how to leash them

I believe in love
I believe in kindness
I believe the universe wants the best for me

It's nice to meet you
I am eager to love you
To start over
To get to know you
To introduce you to who I have become
To fall into forever with you

my favorite flower

Sundays are for sunflowers
The same way roses are for funerals

Our pocket full of posies
Anticipating the fall
Looking for the relief of concrete

Where we find skinned knees and laughter
I don't remember the days too well
But I remember you

With the perfect yellow glow
Of my favorite flowers
In your hands

A smile
A hello
An I love you

A sense of relief
That maybe
Things really will be okay

come home

I want to know
When you are coming back home
I want to have the house ready
Bed made
Sunflowers in bloom
A bouquet waiting for you
I want to mark my calendar
Your name in a bubbled heart
The reunion
To hear the music of your keys
As they dance together
A sound that tells me you are here
You are home
A greeting so long overdue
We will come out
Burnt and overcooked
But still good
A kiss that's been eager to find you
My favorite destination

I want to travel from the tips of your toes
To the ends of your grown out hair
Get there too early
Before the departure
Wait in boarding lines
Window seat for the perfect view
Of you
Detour your hands
To remember
The feeling of being held
Vacation in your ribcage
Sightsee on my way to your heart
Make a pit stop just to say I love you
Take the scenic route to your chest
To lay my head against the safest place I know
Your skin
Will map out my favorite landmarks
Label them with kisses so I can never forget
Every X and O will mark the spot
Of the treasure I call you
A home
So sacred
Not meant for the faint of heart

My favorite place to be
A residence for lovers
A glimmer of paradise in the form of you

when you're home

The moon is my friend
She said
She will light your way back home to me
When you are ready
The stars are my sisters
They said they will keep you safe
As I wait for you
Leave arrows in familiar places
Put up caution signs
Reinforce bridges
Ward off evil

They tell me not to worry
They remind me of the universe
And how she holds you for me
How she wants my arms to have enough room
To carry myself in this time of lonely
She's placed keys inside of us
Doors we will open
When the time is right
When she knows we are ready
For the reunion
The sound of keys
The taste of a longing kiss
The comfort of home
As our threads untangle and shorten
Guiding us back
To a house ready
Bed made
And
Sunflowers waiting

Hotel showers

Used to be home
Of hot water
And sticky skin

Unholy baptisms
A communion
That tasted better on my knees
Giggled wet hums that sounded like hymns

We found heaven in shampoo bottles
We found the holy spirit in between rinses
We found god in each other

Under fluorescent lights
The soap settles
Foggy air keeps us alive
Steamed mirrors—a clock
A burden I did not know at the time

Tubs did not hold us well
The water escapes
Hits the floor
Puddles of us
Begin to evaporate

Towels draped
On skin
The heater kicks on
Dries us off

Your hair starts to curl
I am dressed in your tshirt
We are born again lovers
Died and brought back to life
Purified and resurrected by these hotel showers

I would do it again

Knowing what I know now
Knowing endings are quiet killers
Knowing that you will be the black burning hole inside of me
I would not change a thing
I would still
Find you in the crowd
Smile
Ask for your name
Just to hear your voice again
Fall in love with how the syllables you spoke stuck to me

I would do it in every lifetime

I would
Dip my hands into the volcano
Let them burn
Watch the ash blow in the wind

Grab the ends of the waxy string
Light it on fire
Let the candle melt

Lasso the stars
Let the rope run through my hands
Scar my palms

I would
Crawl through the heavens
Lose my breath in an atmosphere not meant for me
Follow the rivers // the oceans // the lakes
Charm the sunset and the stars
Run into your echo
Let it guide me back to you
Let the strings allow us to stumble back into each other

Where I'll ask for your name
Where it'll feel like we've done this before
Where we'll start over
And do it again

floods

flowers

I've brought you all of your favorite flowers
Placed them on your grave
Peeled the thorns from my fingers
Let the blood become swallowed by the stems
I echo myself into the leaves
Until my voice is a toxic sound
A photosynthesis of unwanted change
The petals sit
Fall stale
Wilted
Atop granite slabs
Housing untold eulogies
And unfinished conversations

I've brought you all of my favorite flowers
Settled them into the tired earth
Begged them to rest
They'll never leave this place
They have nowhere else to go
a cemetery cremation of home
A residence of wishful thinking

I found all of my favorite flowers
On the corner of a familiar street
They meet vases that promise to keep them alive
It is unsettling
How easy it is to trust
Their petals are always the first to go
The water will stop running clear
Dying becomes an overlooked performance
A peaceful sacrifice
They are always willing to make

no, but I got really close

Do not wait
He says
It is unfair
Cruel
How time
Files us down
To bare bone
A chiseled existence
Of unprocessed resentment
In less than kind eyes
An apologetic butterfly effect
That brought you where you wanted to belong
Displaced into cracks of rotten time
Clawing into seconds
Not making a dent
Not making a difference
They remain
As moments

He says it again
The words anchor around me
His heavy harsh reality
Argues with me
He does not get it
Waiting for you
Is meshed into my circadian rhythm
My body is a clock
I am made out of the sands of time
So I will wait
For as long as I need to

arrow slinging angel

Cupid visits me
In all of my dreams
That morph into nightmare
Places pen in my hand
Wishes away my tears
Tells me
        things will get better
        Take it one day at a time
Begs me to keep the pen moving
Promises me love is a carousel
It stays in motion
Sometimes makes us dizzy
But the carnival always comes back to town
So continue to write

But I do not want to write about love
I do not want to write about you
I do not wish metaphors to write this real
When I feel a sloppy soliloquy
Stuttering my way into a puddle of all of the plans we made
The dreams we dreamed
Pockets of promise that are stuck in a queue
Waiting
In lines that refuse to end
Floating in a bottomless void of never going to happen

        I cannot simile my way out of this
        No like or as
        Will carry me to the comparison
        of how much I miss you
        I've stapled all of the euphemisms I could think of to the
        inside of my jacket
            In case anyone asks
            I can read the cue cards
        When my voice cannot come to terms
        It starts to quiver at the thought
        My poems have turned you archetype
            Compartmentalized you
            Sliced you thin

    So that the pain is just a little easier to swallow
        Made you into abstract art
        Because I still cannot understand why

I am a head-tilted observer
Trying to see the picture clearly
I've found hyperboles that feel less like exaggeration
And more like real life
I slip into spells of alliteration
Constantly trying to get to the other side
Seamlessly spilling salty
> Tears
> Telling
> A story of lost love losing its luster
> Leaving me
> Behind
> Blindly believing this
>> Is love

I've told Cupid to take the year off
To stop tiptoeing into my dreams
To take away the pen
I am tired of literary devices holding me
Like I am all that is left
Like I am the only writer with a sad story to tell

But I still find myself
Introducing

> ink

>> to

>>> paper

Like the beginning of the most expected story
Of two people
Who meet
And fall in love

> I still find myself writing another poem
> That will be about love
> That will be about you
> That will be about us

Another set of prose that muffle your name
Lost somewhere in subtle imagery
> But the ending

> Will overflow with more love than I can carry

Dry out my pen
Turn it to sword
So maybe then
Armed with a weapon
You would have fought to keep me

And I would not be caught in contention
with an arrow slinging angel

drafts

I imagine the drafts you type

Then delete

Because you are too stubborn
Maybe too scared
To tell me you miss me too

linger

you live in
    strange places
        in the corner of my collarbone
        in between flower petals of bouquets i refuse to put in water
        in the reflections i catch glimpses of when i do not think
                            I am enough
    in the buttons of a denim jacket that used to hang in your closet

        1 find you often
            Lingering
                without my permission

in dreams

I still meet you in dreams
Find you in fields of sunflowers
Following the petal carpet back into you
An unspoken place we promised to meet
A hiding spot of memories
Where I
        Am a stowaway
        Under the eyes of the glossy moon
        Where the stars watch us fall in love

                every night // again // and always

I am a rosy glow for you
We slip into smiles
Something more comfortable
We laugh a lot
Play giggles like a game
Until sides are sore
An ache I've missed most of all
We exchange stories like currency
I stash my favorites into a jar
To keep me company while you are away
Place these moments on replay

                repeat // until // I feel full again

                        You think it's silly
                        Kind of cute
                        You know
                        I am in love
                        In this dream with you

You smile sweetly
A gesture that makes me run cold
An icy fever dream
You tell me it's time for you to go
I wish
You could stay
You kiss my forehead

                Once // twice // then again
                for good measure // for good luck // for what feels like forever

To make sure I'll remember the feeling
You wish me the safest sleep
Promise to see me soon
I watch you walk away
Dissipate into golden dust
The sunrise wakes me
The tears tell me good morning
Wash me back into a foreign reality

> You are gone
> Until the next time
>
> My eyes grow tired of missing you
>
> And we meet again
> in dreams

film

A roll of film
35mm
Found in a tin box
Left inside a less frequently visited drawer

A polaroid
Exposed to light
Before the shutter
Had a chance to freeze you
Into another memory

The man at the store
Asked about you
I told him you're doing well
The film came back
Nothing developed
The negatives were empty
As if you took the days with you when you left

mourning in the morning

In the mourning
The walls hold in the cold
Like they are afraid it will leave too soon

Stays icy
Because it is familiar

The tea does not warm up as quickly

I drink it cold

Heat rises
It moves past me
Like it has not loved me the last nine years

Finds what is lost
Shoves it in boxes
Shakes the anger away
So they can move forward

I've turned into a shiver
of what you don't want to remember

You cannot stay here
To feel whole
Knowing we are burning holes in the fabric

I hope it was worth it
I hope it makes you sick to your stomach
Wraps you in shame
Because it was too soon
And you knew it

I hope the regret
Reminds you of the mornings we woke up warm
While I am in bed
Heater trying to take the cold out the front door

I imagine the tears you held in
Find their way to the thought of me
Throwing rocks at my window
Hoping
I am still home in the morning

pancakes

I made pancakes in the morning
And found myself crying
With buttered hands and floured face

It's sometimes the small things
That act like chemical agent
A trigger pulled by repressed emotions
Forgotten and stored in a dark corner of the pantry
Dust collected folk tales
Waiting for anyone to listen to the stories of our happy

The same reason vinegar and baking soda cannot hold hands
We react too vividly
Fall apart too easily
Over the tiniest of thoughts

I hope to make you pancakes again
Served with sides of I love you's and sprinkled kisses

For now
I will enjoy my breakfast
Dry up any leftover tears
And place my memories in a to go box for another day

a banana moon

The moon looks like a banana tonight
How stupid
And selfish
And cruel
Can the sky be
To push my thumbs into typing up a message
About the moon playing dress up
On a night
Where missing you
Is like keeping the tide from kissing the sand

How unholy of me
To fall to my knees
Crushed heart and all
Talking to the stars
Like the prayers will make it past the milky way

It is unbearable
How the palpitations
Still beat in a rhythm
That mimics your cadence
Still sings songs
Wanting to match your harmonies
When I am trapped in the chaos
of being too far away from you

The same moon you see
Even over state lines
Shaped like fruit
Already in the past
So much time has passed
Lightyears away from my grip
Still calls me to remember you
As frequently as it visits the sky

pantoum for the Denny's off the 10

They closed the Denny's off the 10
A ritual has died and you never made it to the funeral
Back then you wouldn't mind calling the sunrise home
The nights are shorter the days longer—it was just last summer our hands
held each other

A ritual has died and you never made it to the funeral
I sent you the letters and invitations—hoping death would resurrect your
voice
The nights are shorter the days longer—it was just last summer our hands
held each other
I am doing better
I sent you the letters and invitations—hoping death would resurrect your
voice

I am a dial tone away from losing my mind
I am doing better
I'll drive past the casket building—continuing to mourn the view of you
on the other side of a corner booth

I am a dial tone away from losing my mind
I wish you could have stayed
I'll drive past the casket building—continuing to mourn the view of you
on the other side of a corner booth
They closed the Denny's off the 10

do you miss me too?

Maybe

I wanted to see if you'd miss me
To file down the number of priority

Maybe

I found my answer
I lie too close to the edge
To feel secure in you

Maybe

I wanted to see if you would still search for me
Scroll deep into your archives
Find my name
And tell me
That I am on your mind

But maybe

Maybe

This is too much to ask
To be loved is boarder-line burden to you

Maybe

Wanting to feel important
Is crossing too many boundaries that I don't belong in

Maybe

You really don't miss me

Maybe

I am tired of cementing the ground for you
To walk in a straight path back to me

Maybe

I will stay convenience
Reduce myself into a cushion
Find a crawl space with the scraps you've left for me

Nestle into the reality of wanting more

　　　Maybe
This is as good as it gets

　　　Maybe

This is the love I was destined to die in

persistent

I fell into your arms
For the last time
Persistence has pinned you into a corner
Then dragged you out of loving me
I collapse often
Into piles of unfolded laundry
Into a jacket that smells like your cologne
I fall into arm chairs
That don't hold me back
I am pleading with furniture
On drunken nights
Waiting for sober mornings
To wash the hopeful out of me

weather apps

I still get notifications about the weather
In your city
I hope you brought an umbrella today
I hope the water cycle
Has rinsed you clean
Of all the uncertainty
And the sun makes its way out of the clouds
To find you
Thinking of me
Wondering if the rain
And its bad weather
Started with me
Or ended with you

spring

I am not ready for the spring
                    To call the flowers home
                              To build bouquets
                              You will never hold
          For the setting sun
          To color me orange
          For the purples to reflect in old puddles

          Another season is walking past me
The world is spinning faster than I can run
                    My soles worn out
                    I slow to a sprint
                    Then a walk
                    Now spring is here
                    And I am still
                              not ready

clowns

You say you love clowns
So
here
I
am
Boo boo
The fucking fool
For you
Call me a doctor
Tell the paramedics
I need an AED
Electric shock to restart my thinking
Resuscitate some sense into me
Paint me stupid
And in love
A locked in contractual agreement
To stay here
For x amount of years
However long forever takes
Waiting is the most beautiful curse
A sign of soon
The kiss of one day
The horrors of never
The potential for the truth
Of you never coming home
But I will stay the jester
the comic
the joker
the fool
And the clown
Make a home of my own circus
And remain the punchline

the lighthouse

You used to be my lighthouse
A flash of light to remind me the darkness isn't all that scary
An indication that

I am home
I am safe
I am loved

The day you stopped beaming your glow in my direction
Was the day I had to abandon ship
Life jackets fully fastened
Flares shot into the sky
I looked to be saved
I was blowing the whistle

hoping // someone // anyone// could hear me

We were headed for land
Through rough ocean waves

Currents pushed

Whirlpools pulled

I paddled but couldn't find safety

Instead

we crashed into uncharted sea
All because I couldn't see
Any of the signs or signals that tugged at me
screamed at me
Begged me
to reroute our direction

This ship

Our vessel

Was so deeply damaged
Turned rotten core
And dying leaves

Lacking its luster
Missing its vitality
It begged to be repaired

You were the only beacon of light that I relied on
My own bones didn't trust me
Instead they ached for the warmth of your glow
Like growing pains
They nudged at me to keep drinking from your reserves

Until you were barren
Leaving you an inhabitable heart
Fumes warning you to stop
Still running on empty
All for the sake of me

In your watchtower
You stayed protecting me
As a guide
As a caretaker
Showing me the way home

in all of my darkest hours // my darkest minutes // my darkest seconds

Any time in that darkness
You pulled me out so well

Like this is what you were born to do
But this isn't what you were born to do
I placed you in an occupation
That you never applied to

My love

I am so sorry

To have beaten you down
From pure luminescent perfection
To a flickering flashlight

To have dragged the you out of you

All because I was too scared to be me

Too fragile to be left alone
Too weak to fight my own demons
Too broken to pull my inner child out of her trauma

I hope you know

In the depths of who I am

I am building // crafting // recreating

Rediscovering my own lighthouse
Setting fires where they need to be
Burning a candle that still goes out with a small gust of
wind
I am finding my way out of my own shadows
Preventing them from become the monsters you
battled for me

So take this time to heal from strain
That I've inflected on your heart and
body
Take this time to detach from my darkness
Take this time to remember me in the
light of love
Take this time heal your wounds
Take this time to be your own lighthouse

No longer in our ship
But a lifeboat
I have capsized
One too many times
Without you
But I still sail
Reminding myself

I am home
I am safe
I am loved

a boy and a guitar

I miss the smell of guitar cases
The carpet colored lining
The sound of metal strings dancing between your fingers
Spun together by your voice
A web I miss getting caught in

You were always a muse to the music
All the harmonies knew when you entered a room
They would hum you a welcoming
And when our eyes met
They would settle to a chorus
So they could listen to our laughter
That was more melody than rhythm
You would speak to me in verse
Love me in lyrics
Kiss me to a cadence that would lull me into a daydream

I think you are my favorite chord
I carry trophied callus hands
Just to hear you over and over again
A sound that's been familiar for as far back as I can remember

An acoustic uproar
Still lighting me like a fire
I'd memorize all of your notes like prayers
Hold your promises like hymns
As I sit without you
Nowhere near the music
Nowhere near the metronomes
Nowhere near the guitars strums
That held my hands gently

The sound of you faded
A muted soundscape
A stillness I've learned to befriend
Surrounded by the silence
Now
You are a tempo I can no longer hear

Outloud

if i say

       i miss you

             outloud

      will the syllables travel
               to where you are
will you get a cold shudder

   and think of my icy hands

      does your chest

         still have the same caverns

            that hold my voice

               in an echo

do you listen to it when you miss me
   when the traffic builds
      and the passenger seat is empty
         will the music be enough company

pressed bumper to bumper

    count the telephone poles
      until you are home
        with my voice
           still ringing in your head

rosie

Our wedding song
Played at karaoke

      I did not cry

I don't want them to know
I bit my tongue
Until the blood becomes another cocktail
I had to swallow
Tipsy memories stumble into me
Piledrive my amygdala
Apologizes for the distress

There is an indentation of my teeth on my tongue
      My friends are laughing
      and I can't hear them
They mime me into another joke
The room spins
Like the carnival rides you hated
This time
I become dizzy

The part-time singer on stage
Harmonizes off key
The song is over
I begin to defrost
Become whole again
I unstick myself from phantom arms

      My friends are laughing
      I can hear them
      I can finally
      Laugh with them

hands on fire

This is not the first fire
I will put out
With my bare hands
Look at the burns
Count the degrees
Add them to the seconds
It took my body to tell my brain
This hurts
Please stop
Before my blistered skin
Maps this moment into a memory
Archived into cell membranes
To live in scar tissue
The body's natural ability to heal
The body's natural curse to remember

cigarettes the morning after

I watch you take another sip of beer
                              And wish
                              It was me
                              You could wash down
Like something cheap
And available
                              It'll get the job done
                              I'd get the job done
Mourn the version of me that walked through the door
I'll leave a different person
                              Less whole
                              More desperate

Map out the miscalculated pieces of me
Trace them with your fingers
Press your lips against the achy parts of me
                              Like you are trying to heal them
                              As if I can really find sovereignty
                              In a poorly lit bedroom

Flick away the ash from my cigarette
Romance looks different these days
                              Engage in the small talk
                              Like we always do
Ask about work
Ask how my mom is doing
Ask if I ever finished the book I was working on
                              Dump the ashtray
                              As you walk me to the door
Lean against the doorframe
Tell me you had fun
                              A kiss goodbye
                              An uncomfortable laugh
A pause
                              Because we remembered
                              What this is supposed to be

I had forgotten that love is quick to feel like a dream

I still think about you singing
I still think about the hazy city
I still think about the handshake

    Perhaps

        It was me

        Who met the sun
        The loveliest blinding light
        A flame easy to hold
        A fire that could not find an end
        That melted me whole
        Left me with only ash
        To rebuild
        My palms full of empty soot
        A soft burning reminder

           That everything will be ok

I had forgotten that love is quick to feel like a dream

I still think about you singing
I still think about the hazy city
I still think about the handshake

Perhaps

It was me

Who met the sun
The loveliest blinding light
A flame easy to hold
A fire that could not find an end
That melted me whole
Left me with only ash
To rebuild
My palms full of empty soot
A soft burning reminder

That everything will be ok

kisses

Some days
You kiss me goodbye
Like you'll never see me again
Most days
I believe
You are never coming back to me

i want to, i should

                    I think
          The hardest part
          Is how I don't hate you
    I don't curse your name to the stars
    Hoping the constellations
              will conjure up some well-deserved restitution

          I do not whisper hate into flowered hands
          Petaling lose ends into pulled plants
    I do not hold hatred into silly paperweight thoughts

          Pretty little words

          That song you into my favorite album
                    of a voice
                            I cannot for the life of me
                                  remember
          I echo your voice into the void
          Waiting for returned calls
          That'll stay somewhere I will never reach

          We are not an open casket memory
          But boxed away lovers
          In a dusty closet
          In a crowded garage
                    That sometimes sounds
                    like a heartbeat lost in the floorboards
                            Wanting to be heard

                    I listen

          Until I am a soggy mess on the floor
          Until my eye-ducts ask me
                    to stop turning them into a desert
    When I apologize
    There is never a response
                    So I pray
          To anyone who is up late enough to listen
    I wish your head to be rested well
                    On new pillowcases
                    Fresh bedding
    Blankets that do not linger with the scent of my shampoo
          Silky sonnets
          To twist your curls into a deeper sleep
    Where you do not find bagged luggage
                            next to your bedside

Where you do not wake up with my voice
                              as an alarm clock

The exhaustion
        will no longer be a secret you must keep
Your tongue
        will tell truths your body has already known

                    My hands
                A lover's curse
                Everything I love
                Turns to gold
                  Gold that
                  Cannot
                  Does not
                Love me back

        But
    I will dream of you happy
                Tied to a solstice
                      That tells me you are doing well
                Buttoned to stars
Where you have found pieces of yourself
                                in your own breadcrumbs
                Lassoed to a moon
                That keeps you safe
        Auctioned into the universe
        Where you are loved
        Where maybe
                  You do not hate me either

drowning

I have been drowning myself in poetry
A handmade concoction
Of misspelled words
And off key grammar
Force feeding myself enough stanzas
To fill my already upset stomach

I have been drowning myself in poetry
Hoping it will take me out of this bender
Begging for it to fix me
The same way
They thought bleeding people out would cure a broken heart
Bloodletting was a real medical treatment
Backed by physicians and popes
Forcing out impurities
By cutting veins
Trying to avoid the arteries
Until there was nothing left
But bloody floors
And a pure body
Ready for death

I have been drowning myself in poetry
Cutting out lines
From the back of my throat
Forging the words onto my skin
Until they are memorized
Imprinted as scars
Constant reminders of what brought me here

I have been drowning myself in poetry
The same way
They would puncture maple trees for the syrup
Spilling out slowly
A collection
Of bottled up mistakes
Made out of mourning
To eventually sit on the dinner table
For enough awkward conversations
Make-believe smiles
So they can stop asking you the same questions
As if the tears have not taken you hostage

A few eye drops
To mask the falling apart in your pupils
To bring your irises back to life
I've turned this heartbreak into a flesh wound
Turned you into a tourniquet
Made crutches out of the hands that were meant to hold me
Makeshift and temporary
I still relied on you
To cure the chaos that I've become

I have been drowning myself in poetry
The same way
They tried to turn lead into gold
Transmuting broken into balanced
But I keep falling off the beam
With nothing but my own arms to catch me

I keep drowning myself in poetry
The same way
They thought a camel's brain dried then soaked in vinegar would cure
epilepsy
The same way
They thought electric shock therapy would cure the queer out of you
The same way
They thought eating a mouse twice a month would prevent a toothache
The same way
We hope the bottom of the bottle will bring them back home
When nothing else is working
We find the sane in the insanity
Then call it healing
Stuck in this repetition
Desperation is a disease
Begging is a symptom
That rots you from the inside

So when they do not reply
When they undo the tied knots
When they are not replacing the guilt soaked gauze
When there is nothing left to salvage
When there is only empty space where their love used to be

I have no other choice
But to keep on drowning
Until I learn how to swim
Until I let the water baptize me

Until I learn how to stay still enough to let myself float
Until I turn these poems into currents that can carry me
Safely
Into a cure

sinking

one or the other

I don't know if I am a whisper
Or a faint knock on the door
    I never dreamed to be replaceable
    Or forgettable
I want to be enough
Or worthy of time
    I think my voice is turning echo
    Or muted tones
    Lost to the wind
I wish I knew you could hear me
Or that you were still listening
Ear to the wall
    I want to know if things will be ok
    Or if I will make it out alive
I think I was born an apology
Or a test tube of regret
    Destined for I'm sorry soliloquies
    Or I beg your pardons prologues
    Fated for uncertainty
    Doomed for an upward downfall
But I want to be more than this
A dream too close to the stars
More than memories placed in a safe
    I want to be part of the universe
    A dancer of cosmos
    A collector of planets
    Something
    More than I am

it comes back

It starts with a flicker
Moves into flame
Begins to roar
I remember
I am a furnace
Searing
Forging metals into swords
Anchoring ships to seas
I have always been good enough
My hands bruised with confession
My tears scream I love you's that were too loud for you
Burned you at the touch
A torch
Because
I
am a fire
You
The ocean
Breaking each other apart
Until steam settled
Destined to evaporate
Morphed love into particles
Floating
Existing
Just to take up space
Reaching
Desperate for a sense of being

i'll follow

I feel like I've taken a bite of the tide
And forgot how to chew
I am drowning in all of your empty promises
A tidal wave straight to the face
Like fists for the first time
A salt water rinse
Washes me into a spiral

I am crashing back into the shore that wants nothing to do with me

I feel like I have swallowed the sun
There is something inside me
Burning
Hot and raging
My ribs cracking in the fire
My bones holding it captive
The best they can
There is something ablaze
That I cannot put out on my own
So I hold it tightly
A grip of a desperate ego
If the light goes
I just might follow its direction

the ocean

I've asked the ocean to save me
Wash away the aching in my chest that mimics a broken heartbeat
Cleanse me
With whatever leftover luminescent waves they had left
Purge the ego out of me
Perform the exorcism if necessary
Give me the vision I've been too blind to see
Make me brand new
Baptize me back into nature
From where I came from
Tuck me under the covers
Kiss me goodnight
Let the water sway me out of the nightmares that keep me up

I want to be a glow
The light that lost men follow at sea
Brighter than the stars in the blackest night sky
I want the sun to ask who I am
Engulfed by fire and flame
I don't want to be forgotten
A supernova echoed from
Land
To sea
To the heavens

I've asked the ocean to forgive me
For wanting too much
For being more demand than companion
To see me as more than this human body
Instead
As a river
That finds their way back to something whole
As a lake that freezes in the winter
But comes back to life with the warmth of changing seasons
As a waterfall
That evaporates streams of consciousness back into the atmosphere
A puddle
That begs to be splashed in by the tiniest rain boots

I've left flowers next to my footprints on the sand
Hoping the ocean will know it was me
I wait by the coast

Watch broken glass turn smooth pebbles
Patient for my turn
As the days pass by
I dream to be more than an apology

texas

Everything in Texas is bigger
Not always better
But bigger
The sunsets are somehow both
Bigger and better
Brighter and more beautiful
They tower over you
Like ocean waves trying to capture your image in its own reflection
Mirror all of your hopes and dreams
Placed perfectly
In the palms of your hands

Melodies from the heavens
The sun must have signed a record deal with a deity
With the guidelines specifically stating
"Only in Texas"
No fine print
No repercussions
No deal gone bad
Just a sky brushing its lips against the glow of the residing sun
Nothing compares to the sunsets here in this cowboy infested land
Where good people go to turn red
Where bad people go to burn crimson skin
God had to do something for her least favorite child
Allowed the lone star state to shimmer in shades
Of orange and purple
Dipped hands into golden palettes
And fingerprinted the sky personally
Where we danced
On your roof
Laughed until it was too cold to stay

The sunsets in Texas
Hold you so closely to the heavens
Delicately rock you into a dream
So peacefully soft
You forget you are not home
You forget you are here to mourn
You forget you are parked at a cemetery
You forget the casket is carrying them

looking for answers

Do you think god prays in the middle of hurricanes
Hoping he made the right decisions
Do you think he taps his foot
Walks in anticipation
For time to tell the truth
When hands are folded
Clasped together
Who is he looking to for answers
When the storm finally touches down
Is he afraid of mother nature
A shadow that follows
A creation that does not listen to reason
Who holds him when he is afraid
And no one else is around

happy birthday

It is ok to cry today
When your heart is gift wrapped by your own tired hands
Sticky from the tape and tears
Don't forget the bow
Make it look pretty
Hide behind the confetti and streamers
Blow out your lonely candles
Make the wish
Unrealistic and desperate
Let the oxygen fight the flames
Inhale the smoke
The only warmth your lungs will know today
Save the party hats for next time
Do them a favor
Let the balloons go
Watch them float away
Drift into the space you keep trying to occupy
I hope you remember me today
Still alive
Still breathing
Still dreaming
Somewhere here
Trying to smile and celebrate

pretty

I want to be pretty
A glossy glass image
A prism of rainbow light
Bouncing between four corners
Refracting as your hands hold me
As your fingers press into my cheek
And you call me

pretty

Like it is my namesake
Like it is my birthright
Like it is all you've known me to be

Pretty

Like it's the only home to house me
Where the walls shelve any doubt
Let the dust labor and collect

Pretty

Like the seasons in the middle of change
When dawn doesn't know dusk
When sunrise and sunset dance into something new

And pretty

For once
I'd like to be more than a hand-me-down smile
I'd like the second place ribbon
To be sown into someone else
Pin the consolation prize into thicker skin
For once
I'd like be

Pretty

phantom yearning

It's probably the attention
That paints my brain scans bright purple
That make the screen light up
My toes curl
The butterflies angry moths
Hungry for fleshy skin
When I look down
I remember
I am afraid of heights
I remember anxiety is real
But I also remember
That adrenaline is addictive
And I like this feeling
When you look at me
Like less than a person
But a body to be wrapped in bruised fingerprints
Reminders that you did not want me but needed me
Claw your name into my belly
Kiss the regret out of me
Place your poison into me
Leave me to wake up by a caressing sun
Early into the morning of shame and satisfaction

escape

I like to have men
Wrapped around my fingers
Collapse their lungs with a flick of the wrist
I want to watch them gasp for air
I want the games to feel so real
That even I believe I love myself enough to keep on playing
I want them
To string me along with fishing line
So when I float
The audience believes magic is real
That this is not an illusion
I want to faint into this fantasy
Land on clouds that catch me
When I come to
The blurred vision will be my friend
An ally in the make believe
Shove my sanity in a salt grinder
So I can sprinkle in some sort of contingency
A plan to escape
When I am sick of playing
Sick of being soaked in the dreams of ungodly men
When the panic sets in
I'll remember
The responsibilities of puppeteering
That paying god
Comes with repercussions
A loneliness that does not heal
An empty something I cannot pull off of me
An endless fever dream
Where men wrap me into a forever
I beg to escape from

alcohol to lips

I am everything you want
    And more
Blurring thoughts
Bringing you closer to false enlightenment
Tasting more like oblivion
Bottled telescopes
Trying harder to see the holy grail
Watching it sink to the bottom
Of what feels like an ocean

    I think
    I enjoy the abuse
    I like the way you use me
    I think
    I like how pathetic you sway
    Watching you succumb
    Desperate to feel nothing
        Fall face first

        Resist

    And fail each time
    A hopeless search for sobriety
    The rehabilitation will never take
    I know an addict when I see one

    What does your wife say
    Can you imagine
    The playground conversations
When your children whisper secrets to their friends

        Daddy's
        Drinking
        Again

A framed father who cannot keep it together

    I am alongside you like misery
    Just company
    Light me up and we'll burn

Pitiful

You are nothing but a pitfall
Bracing for impact
Never landing safely
Or in the right place
Always coming back to me
On stressful days
More often on good days
Imagine
How happy you'd be if you didn't need me
How sad
I am the one
To watch you
Die
Slowly
Become more and more lonely
        Tie me like a noose
        Around your throat
        Fly me first class to your liver
        I think
        I am now
        Your only lover

        Pitiful

How I've never loved you in return

butterflies and burdens

I thought that if I did it
I'd come back reincarnated
As a butterfly
Something so small and delicate
A heart as tiny as a thought
Something with the potential to not feel broken
My thoughts would dwell on simple things
Like flying from one flower to another
Do I want daffodils or dandies
A daydream of travel points to get me further than here
Anywhere but here
Just me
The sun
The days
And a future

      I wanted so badly to do it
      But what is the life of a butterfly
      When I have so much I need to do
      Too many poems I need to write
      So much left to be done
      Like love my mom
      Dance with my dad
      And laugh with my brother

A wellness check
Is more of a chin check
With bruising on my ego
A reality check
A sinking ship bringing my heart to the bottom of the ocean
A rain check
Where the door is booming at 3 in the morning
And police are angry at you for wasting their time
Because you are still alive
I thought the confidentiality would stay in the chat
But they found their way to the farmhouse
Where I am being slaughtered for changing my mind
I guess All Cops Are Burdened
When lives are still living
And their hands are still clean

I just wanted to be a butterfly
Flap my wings into better days
Change the narrative
Find my favorite sunset and call it home
Rewrite the story
Pray to God for turning my sanity into sight
And thank the universe that I didn't do it

pink casket

When I die
Whether it be by my own hands
Or gods
Whether the timing is fair
Or gone too soon
I want my casket to be pink and gold
Paint it with the sweetest cotton candy color
So I can dream of the skies I won't see
Dust it with gold
So I can remember golden hour
And all of my golden days

I want to go out like a glitter bomb
You will always find specks of me in random places
Glistening with the sunset on the ocean's bare skin
Blending in with the stars
Call the constellations my cousins
People will make wishes out of me

I want my ex lover to sing all the songs he wrote for me
Even the ones he's never shared
Place memories in speakers
For all the world to taste
I want my friends to write me poetry
Keep me in their journals
Freshly pressed graphite onto paper
Turn me into stories shared on stages

I want to be buried with my parent's tears
Let the salt turn me into rust
Become a placeholder for the grief that they won't know how cope with
I want my brother to know I've looked up to him since the day I was born
I want my sisters to forgive me
And forgive themselves for loving me back too late
I want to be planted on a rainy day
So when the sun comes out
I will come back as a sign from the universe
That I was never truly gone

When I die
Let the ones I love know that I will always love them
Let the other side be welcoming
Let there be a dance party every night
Let the heavens laugh with me

Let death be the joke
Let the dirt be a warm blanket
Keep it cozy
I want the soil to bring me back home

When I die
Plant sunflowers for me every summer
Let my poems be all the comfort they need
When my memory is a lost echo finding its way through the cave
Let my death mean something more than a missing seat at the dinner table

in a past life

I have been told that I was once a celestial body
Glazed with stars so bright
The night sky would become giddy at the sight of me
Guiding nomads to a home they were not aware existed
An almost sanctuary
Crafted by my now brittle bones
My ribs in ruins from holding the weight
Anchored to the ocean floor
I can feel myself drowning
My gravity would pull love out of broken men

I used to beam to the rhythm of pure motherhood
Without bearing children
The goddess inside me was born to nurture
Born to bend and mold
Destined to create life with one gasp of air
But my lungs have failed me
I am heaving just to hold on
To stand my ground
Keep head above water
My sacred heart has been beat like a broken drum
Conducting an off tempo orchestra
A crashing crescendo
A soft spoken sound wave
I am the cause of these casualties
Blood dripped from my bruised up hands

I used to be eternal
A kiss of life would spill from my fingertips
I'd graze the earth and always bring peace

But when you are broken
Even the divine can become cynical
I can feel the darkness reaching for my hand
To take me to the other side of the moon
Where it is icy and destitute
I am falling barren
Life stopped seeping from me
I am begging
Hallowed was my name
But the same existence that I have brought here has turned on me
Pitchforks and a slandered heart

I have forgotten the meaning of celestial
I have lost the ethereal light that made me who I used to be
I am crashing into who I want to be
Refined in who I need to be
Void from being planetary
The fall from grace
An atmospheric phenomenon
I am stuck between layers
Hoping to find myself soon

sea glass

I am sinking
And I do not wish to keep swimming
Let the waves take me home
My body will become glowing reflective pebbles
As they crash and collide with every other broken thing
that resides in the ocean
Smooth out my baggage
Until
I have nothing left but my carry-on
Because I cannot carry on
My eyes remind me that I am tired
When they finally close
They flutter their way into a dream
That will never touch even the edges of reality
My buoyancy keeps me afloat without my permission
I become adrift
Steering into someone whole and real
Water is healing
So she holds me
A little longer than most people
She lets me stay in bed
She accepts my salty tears
She tells me
With time
Even damaged
Discarded
Bottles can become lovely things
She says tumbling is part of nature
Weathered bodies are beautiful ones
She calls me sea glass with a smile in her voice
And stops me from sinking

grandpa

I wish I could remember the color of your casket
The detail in your cowboy boots
Which side your hair was parted
The color of your suit
When I try to think back
The days are blurred fuzzy thoughts
I still cannot grip concept
that the sand is on the wrong side of the hourglass

When my eyes finally come back into focus
The only thing I can hear is your laughter
The reminder that my body is a temple
And god would hate my tattoos
The jokes and cooking advice
Dancing on the roof to Texas sunsets
The phone calls when I was in high school
when you told me that one day you knew I'd find a love that
was real because I was worth it

You always made sure I knew I was worth it
The last thing I ever told you
Was I was going marry to a boy who loved me whole
The joke of a shotgun wedding
That didn't make any sense
But we laughed anyway

You held onto your humor
Like the angles held your body here on earth
Just a little bit longer
Enough for a village of goodbyes

No blood clot could ever take away
your gift of making people laugh
Even in the few days you had left
Your muscles would work hard to make us smile
Putting us first before death
Like a bargain with god
For one more day
The taste of time
Almost bitter
Knowing it will fall right out of our hands

My aunt said
You waited until the very last minute to let go
    And then you did
    And then you were gone
    I was at work
But I knew
    I felt it in the air
    Like pieces of oxygen were missing
    I felt it in my blood line
    Like it hit me
    That you wouldn't be at my wedding
My future children wouldn't ever run into your arms
    I felt it
In every part of me   .
A broken heart unlike any other
                    I sit here
                    Still wishing for so many things

More time // More visits // More pictures // More laughter //

Less pain // Less worry //

A healthier body // A sooner check up appointment // A more thorough
doctor //

                    But mostly
             I am wishing for you

healing

feels like
Laughing with new friends
When you didn't know the sound of it would ever come back
When smiling becomes the norm again

Healing
Feels like blasting every heartbreak song from middle school
Half crying
Half laughing
At preteen you for thinking your heart was really broken at 13
How the lyrics you belted were just
Precursors for today

Healing
Feels like crying in the bathroom of your favorite gym
Because they played Someone Like You by Adele
Why the fuck would they play such a soft song at the gym
I wish I knew
But this is part of healing
You can't keep running from the music
Just because he was your favorite song
He was only a boy with a voice and a guitar
Songs come and go
You can change the station
Find other melodies
Rewrite the lyrics
Let the music be nothing more than music

Healing
Feels like falling apart
Landing face first
In your father's arms
Just to cry
To ask him why you weren't good enough
To ask him what you did wrong
To ask him if it ever gets better
To tell him how much it hurts
To tell him how you don't know if you'll ever get through this

Healing
Feels like becoming more than you thought you'd ever be
Confronting the ideation
Instead of letting it win
Feeling the change in the pit of your stomach
Running to it instead of from it

Finding you in the last place you left yourself
In the middle of a poem
That's begging to be finished
Letting yourself become a dreamer all over again
Breathing in air like the oxygen dared you to

Healing
is loosening the reins
Relaxing your shoulders
Unclenching your jaw
Removing the stitching
Untying the pinky promises
Taking down the pictures
Putting the postcards in a box
Letting objects become just objects
Hallow
Without meaning
Songs are just sounds
Without memories gripping them too tightly

So when I find your contacts
Under the bathroom sink
On a random Tuesday

I will not preserve them
I will not beg them to bring you back to me
I will not turn them ouija board to resurrect old conversations
I will not barter them for a replied lifeless text message
Because I know better
Bringing spirits back to life
Only lingers the haunting
Only elongates the wrong syllables
Puts a dark cloud over the good days
Leaves black smudges around my name
I might not throw them away either
Not yet
Maybe not ever

Healing
is letting go

Memorializing you into poetry
Keeping your heart on my sleeve
Time stamping you onto my skin

To remember // You were real

To remember // You loved me
To remember // It will get better
To remember //This is healing

reoccurring dreams

When I dream of you
There are no clouds
Or rain
Just the rays of the sun
Pressing against my skin
A warmth that only you know how to bring
A laugh that comes with the breeze
Infectious and lighthearted
Safe and loving
Always tender
Like forgiveness was on the edge of every smile

No distance or time placed us in confined spaces
You are here
Cowboy boots ready for Sunday's best
Not a hair out of place
Grays and all
The pillars of your church know you well
I think they dream of you too

When the air is dry in California
I think of Texas
The drive that counts too many miles
When I see horses
I think of your farm
The one I never got to visit
My uncle says his cousin owns it now
Repeats
At least it's still in the family

When you visit
Everything is okay again
My dad still has his dad
And does not cry to me
When he cooks any of your recipes
There are no cobwebs collecting
On your windbreakers
And your silver watches still tick
Like a reminder that time is a thief
And not a good one

Swimming

perhaps

Maybe if I smile long enough
My face will get stuck
Like my parents warned me it would
Maybe the permanence
Will strike the match
My body needs
To remember
How to brace for impact

heat

This is the fire you asked for
A ruptured lung inside of an embered body
A volcanic temper
Fuming
Breaking the gates
Carving into raging ground
Pressing magma into places it does not belong
Unsuspecting ground will crumble
This is the rapture
You begged for
Dirty boots
Batons glazed in dried sticky blood
These are the smokey eyes
You've yearned for
Red and burning
When bodies become charcoaled piles
Do not look for fertile land
On horizons you set ablaze
Do not cry over spilled gasoline
When the earth does not forgive you
Remember that this
Is the fire you asked for

ask before you hug

Can I be honest

I
Fucking

      Hate
Hugs

My body is already uncomfortable
As in my existence is questionable
To be seen as whole and unbroken
To be held
By so many hands
Gripped by a loving embrace I might not deserve

In these small moments
It feels like suffocation
Seconds mutate into a time warp
A distorted never ending grip
Gasping for it to end quickly and quietly
I pretend I can stand it
I pretend I've earned it
I pretend I don't need it
I will smile through them all
Just to be polite
To follow the protocol
Exchange the pleasantries
With a side of uncomfortable small talk
A tortured textbook social requirement

I see it coming
Like I've predicted my own death
Planned my funeral
Wrote my own eulogy
So I cringe
And I ache
In the quietest parts of me
When I see the arms
The gestures
The open invitations
For another hug
For the call and response
The result of their body

And my body
Parallel in my space

Scents stuck to the fabric of my favorite cardigans
That I will over wash
Until the seams are screaming for air
I don't want the smell of strangers lingering
Illuminating me
Haunting reminders that I've done it again
Placing good manners before myself

blessed are the homies

Blessed are the homies
That fake a phone call
To get you out of a bad situation
Text a quick code word
No hesitation
No questions
To play it safe
They've memorized their lines
Just in case it has to go on speaker
They read from the script
A play
I like to call
How to not get murdered for rejecting a man

Blessed are the strangers
That go along with you
When you run up to them
A nervous giggly smile
A "hey! I was just looking for you!"
The panic in my eyes
Read like a teleprompter
The pretend we have to play
To stop being followed
To get from point A to point B
Alive

Blessed are the friends that keep bats in the trucks of their cars
That take on the job of bodyguard
Without pay
Without benefits
Without time off
Without anything in return
But a friend who can enjoy a space
Without worrying
About laced drinks
About weirdos
About creeps
About entitled men that think you owe them a second of your time

Blessed are all of the no's
I have to shove inside of my pocket
Zip into my purse
Swallow without water

I wish you were a word
I did not have to constantly whiteout of conversations
I wish you were easier to keep around
I wish you were a more powerful single syllable word
I wish you weren't a trigger
I wish you didn't have accompany you with apology
Because I
am not sorry
I am not interested
I am being polite
I am uncomfortable
I am usually scared
Because I came here to dance
I came here to watch the band
I came here to write
I came here to shop
I came here to put gas in my car
I am here for coffee
I came here to have a good time
I came here for myself
I came here just to be here

Instead
You are wasting my time
Staring at me
With a barrel of a gun as eye contact
As I am listening for the buzz of neon exit signs
Counting the doors
Wondering if the windows slide or lift
I am looking for all the ways I can escape
All of the ways you can stop me
All of the ways you can take my tomorrows
And bury them somewhere in a ditch right next to my body
Where there are be signs of abuse
And torture
And force
Signs that I fought back
But still lost

I've had enough experience
I've heard enough horror stories
And whispers
Warnings to not take the trips on your own
To be careful
To take your pepper spray
To place keys in between your knuckles
To have 911 pre-dialed
To stay in sight of CCTV cameras
To have your location on
To have shared your passwords and log-ins with someone you trust
Just in case

We walk around their invasive behavior
Let them continue to be openly intrusive thoughts
Arm women for the just in case
Take classes on endless preparation
Instead of teaching men to just be better
We are living inside a "just in case" glass bottle
That could break so easily and out in the open
So suddenly and seamlessly
So obvious and blatant
The media will still quote my family saying
"we never saw it coming"

I have become another name at another funeral
Where I am blessed to be in a better place
Blessed that I am no longer suffering
These blessings are bandaids
Mantras we are forced recite
Blessed are all of the women
Who continue to live as caution sign
Blessed are all of the women
Who stay home because they are too afraid
Blessed are all of the women
Who fight back
Blessed are all of the women who survived
Blessed are all of the women who didn't make it
And death
To all the men
Who are the reason they are not here

my american tongue

My parents weaponized language
When I would enter a room
Code switched too quickly for me to understand
The adults are talking
They spoke softly just in case
In a vernacular I can only dream of
I grew bitter to be detached from my heritage
How do you say spiteful in Spanish
I grew up angry at my culture
Like I wasn't good enough to know them personally
Like I didn't belong here
And that was their fault
Like it was a bully
And I was an easy target
Bulls-eye dotted pupils
Always anticipating the arrow
The insults
What do you call a Mexican who cannot speak Spanish
My aunt said a coconut
Brown on the outside but white on the inside
But I can't even fill in those shoes
Because my skin decided to be unfair
And burn in the graces of the sun instead of tan
How do you say identity crisis in Spanish
Maybe I wasn't strong enough to carry the weight of my ancestors
To be kissed by a dialect passed down from one generation to another

In high school
I took French
Like a fuck you to Spanish
I took that shit personally
A vendetta engraved in me
Maybe that way she'll learn her lesson of staying secret
And talking behind my back
Maybe that way she'll feel the damage of being outcast

Instead she would conjugate into shame
Corner me into an inferiority complex
When I hear my grandmother fight through the complexity of English
Just to say I love you
Just to ask how my day was
And understand me when I responded

The barriers came straight from my own hands
Digging the distance deeper and deeper
How do you say I was wrong in Spanish
How do you say I am sorry in Spanish
How do you say I don't know who I am in Spanish
How do you say I don't know who I am supposed to be in Spanish

I can't tick enough boxes to call myself Mexican
without the discomfort of non-believers
Except on applications
But mostly because of my last name
A name given to me by father
A name that tongue ties me into embarrassment
Because I still cannot roll my r's properly
Without sounding like I've bleached my tongue white
My accent never developed
Played hide and seek with me and won
My ancestors look away in shame
They don't know how I slipped into their lineage
I lack a lot in tradition
Fall too short in customary design
I have to hyphenate American after Mexican
That's the only way they'll believe me
Like I am branded with the burden
Of never being enough
Always and forever asking
How do you say it in Spanish

He brings guavas
In an old grocery bag
To the after-school program
For his girls
He pushes the swinging door
Forcefully
There are hints of aggression in his footsteps
I stop him in the office
With the most understanding voice I can find
This is not the first time
We go over the rules yet again
Yet again he is angry at the response
Because it is unfair
It is not right
He says we know him
But we don't really know him
He is just a grown man trying to enter school grounds
And it is my job to stop him
My job to tell a grown man *no*
Then watch him throw a fit

He tells me none of it is his fault
He blames the city
Says Pomona is not a good place
Tells me the city poisons its people
That's why he doesn't drink the water here
He blames his wife
Says women from this town
Don't know how to pick a good school
He blames the district
Says they can't hire good teachers
Like me
I smile
More out of discomfort
More out of pity
To watch a father
Made askew
Made a fool
As he becomes defensive
Combative to his rights
"I am their father"
"I am a man of God"

A roar from a broken man
Like those words would be enough to let him in

He makes demands like he is holding onto hostages
Hoping they could heal him
Anger turns desperate
He begins to beg
A primitive pleading
He brought them food
A basic necessity
Guavas on Mondays
Picked from grandma's backyard
French fries on Tuesday
Fresh from the corner of Holt
The best for his babies
He just wants to give them something to eat
To fill their bellies
A way to make them feel special
Give them stories to tell
That daddy was a good man
That daddy tries his best
That daddy loves them the most
He wants to see their smiles
To kiss the top of their heads again

He tries to fight his way on campus
Through the gates
Past the noon aides
In the middle of
"Sir you can't be here"
He cuts them off
Rolls his eyes
Mumbles some obscurities
An untreated condition
He continues to march
A storming of the castle
If he reaches the lunch tables
He knows he's won
He can see them
He is so close
To gifting them another piece of love in food form

With an audience of confused students
During snack time
They are unaware of the magnitude
This defining moment
They watch him
Escorted away
Unaware of a splintered family

Chipped smaller and smaller
Pieces of wood are left behind
Deep under the skin
Of his girl's fingers
An invisible wound
An ache they can never seem to reach
Or mend fully
Something that is stuck there
For what feels like an eternity

When it hurts the most
When there is a phantom throbbing
Their stomachs will growl
They will crave guavas
From grandma's backyard
When they drive past the McDonald's on Holt
In the midst of a foreign anger
A hunger they've met before
They will smell the fruit in the breeze
Feel grains of salt underneath their fingernails
A gentle wind taps into their memories
A reminiscent moment
They will miss the voice of their father
Wince at the strangest feeling of pity
Never putting the pieces together

not a place for guns

It is built into our schedule ahead of time
I mark it on my calendar
Pencil it into our day
Highlight it into my agenda
Alarm clock it into my phone
Just so it does not catch me off guard
Even when I know
Even when I have planned
And practiced
Rehearsed the drills
The conversations
How to hold back tears to the reality
That though not often here
It could always be us

They rather have us safe than sorry
Over prepared rather than panicked
Caught in routine rather than dead and bloody
9:15
The announcement goes off
My assistant principal sounds almost robotic happy

This is a lockdown drill
This is a lockdown drill
Teachers follow lockdown procedures

My kids
They run
Scurry so fearful
But giddy like this is just another game
Scarlett shuts off the lights
Chromebooks slam closed
Ethan checks the window
In our silence
I stand by the door
Like bodyguard
But what can my body really do to protect my kids
Other than human shield
And first victim

I watch the seconds on the clock mock me
Our principal bangs on our door
shakes the handle
I know it's not real
But I can feel the safety leave my body

In a breath
My hands
They shake
I question how we have even ended up here

I am jerked back into reality when I hear
Table 3 starts to giggle
Table 5 shushes into place
Table 1 begins to talk
I can feel the frustration bubble
Gurgling inside me
I need them to know this is more than practice
This is not a game
We are not playing pretend
Bullets do not care who you are
I want them to stop talking
But they are just kids
This is just a drill
So I remind them
Voice level zero friends
take it seriously friends
another reminder friends

There is a chime
Then a lull
The robotic announcement taps us on the shoulders
The lockdown drill is over
And we are supposed to go about our day
like this is part of our norm
Now second nature
To know how to train 2nd graders to weaponize textbooks
Build forts out of desks
Show teachers how to jam doors closed
How to fight for lives that have not fully lived
To be willing to sacrifice our own bodies
When we still have plans of our own
How to tiptoe around the conversations
When Eli asks
Why do we have so many windows, won't they see us?
Jacob questions
Would desks really keep us safe?
Ezra asks
What do we do if it happens when we are on the playground?
Charlotte comes to me at recess
Asks why someone would want to hurt us at school
Her eyes so full of worry
I wish I could bag it up and take the burden far away from her

She stays lost in thought close to me
When she should be playing four square or tag
Not jump roping around the thoughts of what if

I like to be prepared when I play brave for my kids
I like to build the reality that we will be okay
Feed them the reassurance that I would do anything to keep them safe
I think of my own mom and dad
I apologize out loud
Because I know
I would do anything to keep my kids safe
But I am running out of answers
I am fearful of the hope I hold onto that it'll never be us
I am scared because I did not think my profession
As educator
As teacher
Would include rounds of bullets aiming for innocent bodies
For reasons that will never be enough

boys will be boys

We just have to sit and let it happen
Take it on the chin
Barbie smile and grin
Bat our eyes
Play homemaker
Wifey material
Pull the string on our backs
So we can repeat our lines
Stand up straight
Suck in our stomachs
Speak correctly
In the perkiest tones
Remind us we are gatherers and not hunters
Force us to bend over
Backwards
Give and give and give and give
In a dream house we never asked to part of
With a list of mannerisms we didn't sign off on

But it's fine
It's cool
It's all fucking good
Because you know
Boys will be boys
And they will grow up to be
Men that will be men

Men that will be men
With the audacity
The bold in their step
The fearlessness
And lack of repercussion
No capacity for empathy
With the inability to understand consequence
To sink their claws into my skin
Without permission
Without warning
But with all the excuses
Nudged into
"I was just messing around"
"Why are you taking it so seriously"
"You should be so lucky"
Lucky that I was that night's prey

Sliced up tv tray dinner
Left grimy and half eaten
By big bad wolf–
Man
I should have known
I should have been prepared
His eyes said he owned me the second we made contact
Inked me full of uncomfortable
A shock down my spine
In the pit of my intuition

Why don't I get a say
That this is my body
Not a tester on display
Get your hands off of me
Get your hands off of me
Get your hands the fuck off me
But my voice is just a popped bubble
Gone and incoherent

But it's fine
It's cool
It's all fucking good
Because you know
Boys will be boys

We've deemed it excusable
Because we let the boys be boys
A false reality of what boys should be
We spoon fed them power over people
Said it's okay
It's just a body
Not a person
Take and take
And take and take
Whatever the fuck you want
Innocence
And land
And jobs
And time
And dreams
Whatever the fuck you want
And society will laugh it away
Give it a tax write off

Because it's just boys being boys
But tell me what is the age limit
Where do we draw the line
I don't want to keep feeling guilty
Holding onto shame like companionship depends on it
I don't want to have this confession riding on me
As if I committed the crime

Look my father in the eyes
When he asks me what happened
Find the strength inside me to admit
Someone's claws plunged into me
Desperately
When I didn't want it
And apologize
On this man's behalf
Like I am vouching for him
Continuing the cycle of letting boys stay boys

But it's fine
It's cool
It's all fucking good

fan fiction fantasies of men

I have an iPhone
With iMessage
The blessed blue bubble
Updates that outdate the newest version of me
A fragile glass screen
That reflects too much I don't want to see
The future in my palms
The technology of tomorrow

But sometimes
I hate my phone
Because with all the futuristic possibilities
It's become a hellscape
The doors to the dungeon
That leads me the brimstone
Full of fuckbois
And names saved in my contacts
Where I have to place a description in order to remember who they were
like

> Guy from club
> Guy who talks way too much about creatine
> Guy from bookstore
> Guy with stupid pants
> Guy ??? with a bunch of questions marks
> Guy with weird shirt
> Guy with just a phone number because he wasn't worth a name
> Guy with cute accent
> Guy who was an asshole but wrote me poems

Names I should have deleted a long time ago
Names that are followed by the skull and crossbone emoji
A warning I continue to take lightly
Like I did not learn the first time
Like I did not learn the second time
Like I did not learn that last time

I have a catalog
Of shitty nights
Categorized them
Created my own Richter scale
My version
Where I determine their level of destruction on my value

How my tectonic plates are being rubbed the wrong way
How they can never find my epicenter
How they're cracking my foundation
How I am still waiting for the big one
How I am at fault
Because I let them

I keep finding myself
With my head laying on pillows without silk cases
Of people who will forget my face
In beds I will never be familiar with
Next to nightstands that are on the wrong side
With a hunger
That does not go away
An appetite
That does not know how to be satisfied

And the messages
Full of obnoxious amounts of fire emojis
What that mouf do
Nudes? lol
Baby I can show you a good time
You look like you're good in bed
Bullshit one liners
Are the only things these men can offer me
That make my eyes roll back
Genuinely
Fuck your dick pix
Pix with an x
Because you've shown me
How you can't spell
How grammar is not your friend
How looks don't always outweigh personality

I am tired
Of these tall tales that come from a poor man's wet dream
My hands are over typing the same old thing
lol you're so funny
lol yeah it was good
lol it's huge
lol no yeah I came too
Sick of feeling nothing
Sick of the uncomfortable
Sick of saying let's do this again sometime

Sick of being so self-destructive
Sick of these fantasies
That were never mine

to the children I will never have

My body is more chaos than temple
A sanctuary in ruins
Crumbling at its core
It is not safe here
It is too anxious
To hold you steady
My bones too brittle to carry the weight of both of us
In a belly that was never meant to be a home

I wanted you to live here

A permanent residence
On earth
    With me
        In my arms
But there is too much fire and flame
A burning building
On the verge of collapse
A roof housing nothing but ash
    And death
Crumbling at the touch of my hands
Drowned in smoke inhalation
Your lungs never had a chance
I will never be strong enough for us

This vessel

Lacking in the capacity for life
Predestined for a desolate body

I wanted to be a home for you

A shelter on cold and windy days
Your favorite smile in the sun
The warmest hugs you've ever known

I need you to know
That I have always dreamed of you

I know your eyes
Are bright and bold

You would have been brave enough to do all of the
   things I was too scared to do
You have always been more fearless than I could ever

I would have taught you so many things
Everything I never got the chance to learn
How to get out of bed on hard days
To keep on trying
Mistakes are beautiful
               Your dreams are worth it
               Some people really
               really suck and that's ok
               There is still good in the world
               In small places
                    I promise
                    Love is real
                    But it hurts
                    And sometimes
The hurt is what you were supposed to know all along
          Like this ache of not having you beside me

They told me
I would have loved you
too much
Suffocated you with my fears of letting go
Drained the happiness from your heart
Dulled any sparkle left in you
It's all I've ever been known to do
Turn dreamers into dust
I am a routine cycle of devastation
An apologetic voicemail left unheard

               A body

               A vessel

               A host

          Not meant for this
          Not meant for you
               I break all that I love
          Effortlessly
          But know

I would have

Never

Broken you
Never dared to give you fragmented slivers of love
Even my bad days would've been your good days
I would break every single generational curse
In a heartbeat

You would have been safe here

Nothing would have ever tainted your skin
All of my fears gone at the very first sight of you

You would have been happy here

For you
I would have been anything
And everything
You ever needed
I would have been more than this tired body
Turned the chaos back into temple
A skeleton framework
Made just for you

A life giver

My stolen birthright

A mother

And I'll still visit the thought

Bury myself in hopes and star sent dreams
Where I will meet you in every rainbow
Kiss you where the sunset meets the ocean
Carry you in all of my whispers
And call you home to me every night

microaggressions

Micro
As in small
Or reduced in size

        Aggression
        As in hostile
        Or violent behavior toward another

Funny

How nowhere in either definition does it say
That phrasing racism in joke form makes it ok

Funny

How it is synonymous to violence
But minimized
Whispered in an undertone
Curious
Who decided
To dilute hate crimes into a minor offense
To shrink an experience into a so-called comical remark
Like this is routine
Normal behavior

Maybe

Maybe you didn't know
So here
Here is the benefit of the doubt
Take it

Or maybe

You know exactly what you were doing
Begged my eyes for an approval
Like if the only Mexican in the room laughs
        Then it's ok
        You're safe
Not judged
Or placed in a box
Not feeding into the problem
Off the plate you hand served yourself

Ignorance is bliss
And you are blissful in its entirety
The epitome of elated
Even when it is performance based
A one-sided point of view
The "humor" tip toes on the bodies of smaller people
Keeping us in the margins
Where we belong
A place we know best
Out of the way
Displaced as foreign colonies
That you like to call the punchline

Funny

How the truth slips out
A caterpillar from a distorted cocoon
Revealing how transparent true intentions are
Your racism is showing
I must've missed my cue
Not even a chuckle christened from my lips

It wasn't funny

I don't want to swallow bigotry
Like another societal pill
I refuse to be put down by another
       Unsalted
       Unflavored
Uncle Tom conformative blonde body

It was only a joke
Everyone else laughed
When she made fun of the way I said the name of my city
Told me how to pronounce a word that's never touched her american soil t
Asked me why I said it like that
Turned me small and frail

Questioned who I was trying to impress
La Puente
Is where I am from
La Puente
Sorry I mean La Puente (La pwen-knee)
Sorry I mean La Puente (La pwen-tee)
Sorry I mean La Puente (La pwen-tay)
Had me second guessing what I've always known as home

Had me calling my mom on my drive back to the bridge city
Trying to retrace my steps
To see where I went wrong

Only to realize
It was your privilege
That was holding my head underwater
Dousing me in an identity crisis
Letting me light the flame of my own cultural demise
Bathed kerosene
The fumes of her fire
We played an unfair game of you were right and I was wrong
So you can sit comfortably in your prejudice
Like you are not the pit of the problem

Funny

How she will continue her patterns
Make a quilt of fake equality
Her teachings will go on
In young children to follow
To let them think
These jokes are just jokes

for natalie

Home is a belly
Where miracles happen
Life is making its entrance
Made from scratch
Each ingredient precisely poured
From hands that hold nothing but love
You
Are being formed
So perfectly
Etched in the image of God
From a heartbeat to fingernails
You
Keep on growing
The thought of you is bright
A glowing piece of hope
A dream kissing reality
When we talk about you
We can't help but smile
You've turned happiness
into something tangible

She dances
Just like her Mother
She tumbles and turns
A ballerina
At the sound of a voice she knows as Daddy
I know she tallies the days until she gets to see him

Your parents are dreamers
They know love like the back of their hands

When they hold you for the first time

They will get a glimpse of heaven
A taste of the promised land
Witness the art of God
Nothing else will matter
But you
Only you
Forever
A dream turned real for the dreamers

9/30

My bangs are too long
So I cut them
Then cry
When they are too short
I've turned this into ritual
Where my hands bleed
For all the versions of me
Chipped away with scissors
The hair was already dead to begin with
But I mourn
I cry
I cannot bring back to life
Who I could have been
If I let my hair grow any longer

truths about the teacher's lounge

There are no mystic magic clouds of wonder

That lead you to the holy grail of answers
        No gold or rainbows
        No unlimited rivers of youth
        No pearly gates
        No liberation of corporate America
There aren't even vending machines
Only routine conversations about the day fog
Of keeping too many students accountable
        Safe
        Engaged
        And on task
Answering questions

            Repeating directions
                        Repeating directions
                                    Repeated directions

Remembering too much all at once
While crashing into chairs that are not pushed in
Tripping over wires
Despite the reminders
        And repeated directions
Never mind the expectations

                But
If you can just remember your "why"
You can convince yourself
You can get through another day
Of out-of-contract responsibilities
Donuts for your hard work
Paid out of pocket spirit wear
Jeans on a Friday

When you return to the teacher's lounge
After recess duty
With barely enough time to breathe
Let alone pee
You will meet more achy eyes
The united agony and solidarity
        Of teacher tired
                We forge smiles back into frame
                March into the trenches
                Where the pins and needles have already broken skin

Where admin is ready to waste more time
With a meeting that should have been an email
Where parents reach the conferences
                without smiles or understanding
                a fist full of 'this is your fault'
You can see apples stay close to the trees
Dragged by roots that can never stay rooted
But poison the soil instead
Leaving us to blame for the bad fruit

But some rumors are true
Sometimes the laughter muffles the drowning
The tears never help us stay afloat
But that doesn't stop us from crying
The life jackets are always defective
The whispers were right
We are the proprietors of fatigued compassion

        Teachers

            Are

                Tired

Of pencils unsharpened
Of having more students than desks
Of administration that twists the knife of pressure
Into exhaustion
Parents without patience
But a list of demands

What is one more unpaid task
What is another underpaid overqualified professional

        We are tired

Of loans more expensive than a salary could pay
From universities that did not prepare us for the reality
Of empty government funded classrooms
Strangled wallets
Split paychecks
That fill barren backpacks
And sometimes lonely bellies
Of students who don't want to go home

        We are tired

Of assessments that tell us we don't care enough
That we don't teach well enough
That we are never going to be good enough
Tests that don't reflect the focus of my student's well-being over a score
An assessment that doesn't show the late hours
The worry
The middle of the night panicked idea of how we can help our students
The work that follows us home
Haunts us at the dinner table
Steals us from our families
Everything we go home with
Takes a toll
Burns us into a frantic flame trying to continue to stay lit
    Teachers
        Are dropping like flies
            Barely making it back to the teacher's lounge

3 things I learned from a girl who constantly
claimed to be a girl's girl

1 when a girl feels the obligation
              to continuously claim she is a girl's girl

       She is probably not a girl's girl

Any inclination to hijack a conversation about the one time
She didn't flirt with some else's boyfriend
Should have been red flag number one
When she has the endless urge
                    to prop her pedestal in front of you

                         Making you feel small
                         Unimportant
                         And overshadowed

       It's time to cut the ribbon to this new friendship
       The grand opening was too excessive anyway
       You have become too accessible
   The side door entrance to what she really wanted out of you

                  She practiced her lines
                  Painted her face as friend
                  A misleading smile
       To make you believe in the safety of her conversation
              She prepped and prepared to take over

                         A replacement
                         A substitution

         But she is a malfunctioned model
                  Cross-wired
                  Defective and faulty

                  The audacity to think
              She could ever step into your light
           A case of cinderella stepsister syndrome
      She can never cut enough of herself to fit into the slipper
                 That has always belonged to you

2 love bombing in friendship can be paralyzing
       It's easy to be blinded by an expert
Masking her fallacies in gifts and kind words
She is lacking in merit

All of her badges are counterfeit
Being too trusting is your fatal flaw

This friendship was killing you

She plays leech so well
Sucking the life from you
To keep herself grounded in her own make-believe
Snakes will always be snakes
Moving almost motionless
Maneuvering through lives that are cracked

Slowly chiseling at your foundation
To create the life she craves so desperately
Making a fort within your insecurities
Playing friend when she is fraud
She is weakening you from the inside
So silently that you will never hear your own warning sirens

3 stand your ground
When you finally find pattern in her step
Play her game strategically

Do not let her bullshit live peacefully

Make your presence known
Walk with purpose

She is too old for this fuckery
Old but not grown
Incapable of the confrontation

As you enter
Allow fear to guide her own suffering

Fuck this "bestie I'm a girl's girl" bullshit

Let her seep into her own mistakes
Drown in the damage she's created
Lean into the clichés
Because her misery loves your company so deeply
She will walk away like this heartache cracked her to the core
Have no sympathy for her
She's felt no sorrow for her chaos
Let her rain clouds be her only friend

Let her step to the side in hallways
Make room for your command
Quiet her voice when you speak
Without any words
She will feel the intensity of your being

She will see that this was the wrong person to play girl's girl

brown v board of ed

They say
Times have changed
That we are so far left
We can't see the right
Side of history
That we've made enough progress
The nation is healing through the chaos
But these trying times
Never seem to be trying hard enough

In 1954

It took nearly 2 years

730 days
For the Supreme Court to rule unanimously
on Brown v. the Board of Education

Finally deciding

It was unconstitutional to separate children in public schools on the basis
of race
Stating it was in violation of the 14th amendment

After the 2 years

After the 730 days

It still took over a decade for schools to desegregate fully
We've tried to drag the racism out of the laws
But could not pry the racism out of the people

In 2024
Supreme Court Judge
Clarence Thomas
Wanted to repeal the decision of Brown v. the board of education
Said the ruling was an overstep
Said it used too much judicial power
Thought we were heading down the wrong path

He
is a roach in the community
A slimy after thought
That does not use his power for the greater good

A jack with no trades
You do not want in your hand
A joke
Yet
He resides
On a panel
That makes decisions for people
Whose voices are zip tied in the back of a caged van

In the 2023-2024 school year
My former school district
Argued endlessly at board meetings
Then finally put into place a policy
That forces teachers
To out their students
If they ever decide
That their gender is foreign prison
That held onto who they were meant to be
In chained bodies
If they found their truth
In a new identity
Boundless of gender

We, teachers

Had to notify parents and admin immediately
Taking their trust and safety
Folding it into paper planes
Sending it
Out the window
Into homes
That I can only pray are safe enough to hold them new
Into homes
I am begging to love them whole
This policy has brought a new rage out of me
I am boiling over into a new millennium
They thought we'd give up our students this easily

It seems I've brought basic human rights to a gunfight
And they've brought fear into elementary schools

Our students
Our children
Our kids
Remind me
Every day

That I love what I do
That they are more than a statistic
More than test score
More than a body in a chair for the state to get another dollar and dime
We don't educate them into conformity
We teach them how to be kind
We teach them to love who they are
We teach them to fall in love with learning
We teach them to know their rights
We teach them to advocate for themselves
We teach them to speak up for others
We teach them how to protest peacefully
We teach them how to protest safely
We teach them to never stop fighting
We teach them that we might have the luxury to ever stop fighting

In 2025
President trump
Tries to remove sanctuary in schools
Allowing ICE to turn campuses into frozen stomping grounds
To peel parents out of their child's arms
At the dismissal gates
When the bell rings
They sound more like warning sirens
Telling parents to find new pick-up arrangements
To stay out of sight
To hold their babies
Just a little bit tighter
For little bit longer

I don't know what type of post-apocalyptic bullshit world
we are living in

But it is failing our children
Placing curses on our future
Painting the city red
With bodies
And hats with slogans
The incite riot gear and panic
When the skin does not match the agenda
When the conformity strays off the chosen path
When the big man is insulted
When the CEOs salute and we do not cheer
When do not give up our kids
as easily and they thought we would

These trying times
Are tiring
These trying times
Are really trying me
These trying times

Are still

Not trying hard enough

me, my dad, and baseball

Sometimes I wonder
What my dad dreamed
when he thought about having children
If he imagined balance
A solid ratio

I wonder
If my dad ever wished I was a boy
A friend for my only brother
To even the odds
In our games of make-believe
If he wished his girls
To be less girly
Less dainty
And frail

    I have photographs
    of my old man
    Baseball uniforms
    Teams and bats
    Jersey numbers and trophies
    He tried to get me to play softball
    Bought the mitts
    In pink
    My favorite color
    All the more enticing
    Said we could paint the bat too

We practiced in the yard
Woke up too early
My siblings still in bed
Tried to live out what felt like his dream
Him and his favorite girl
A baseball daughter
Running circles around bases
Making it home
A cheering crowd
A proud father

    My dad tried to teach me guitar
    Wanted me to love the music
    The way he did
    To be a dreamer
    To know the classics

Said he'd teach me himself
He learned by ear
Practiced for hours
Got good
He knew I would too
Told me my fingers are long enough
to dance keys into songs

We practiced in the living room
After a trip to guitar center
He showed me how calluses are proof that it's working
Played my favorite songs
Taught me what a chord was
Said I don't need to know how to read music
I could just play
I would hear it
And feel it
And know it
Like he did

> My dad wanted me to be an accountant
> The day I told him
> I was destined for a classroom
> Born to be a teacher
> He said
> It wasn't where the money was
> I reminded him
> I was bad at math

We never practiced
I only cried
When my math homework
Started making less and less sense
When letters and numbers were in the same equation
And he couldn't help me

> My first guitar lesson with my dad
> Ended in an argument
> Our temperaments made the worst sounds together
> My fingers would always slip
> Losing my balance on each fret
> Mixing major keys for minor chords
> I couldn't hear the difference in any of the sounds
> I never got good
> Like he did

I never had a first baseball game
Never tried out for the team
I've only engraved disappointment
into the wood of a faded pink bat
I was always too soft to play
The sun in my eyes
Scared of getting hit
Afraid of the ball
More afraid of being a disappointment
I've always been bad at sports
Always good at falling short of my dad's expectations

I never became an accountant
Barely got better at math
My dad loves that I am a teacher
Laughs at the lists of instruments
We wasted money on
Lost count of the arguments and
Slamming doors
'The dinner's ready' apologies
With my favorite meal

Last year
I fell in love with baseball
I wear a dodger's jacket
The same way he wore his uniform
I imagine
That my dad
Sitting next to me
Drinking a cold beer
In the California sun
Listening to the 7th inning stretch
Was more than he dreamed

Though the mitts
Not pink
Though the guitars collect dust
And the math overlooked
He does not think of me
Girly
Dainty
Frail
But full of grit
Someone who became something
More than a parent's expectations

Photo by: Alicia Valle

Author Bio

With roots from the small city of La Puente hidden somewhere in
the San Gabriel Valley, Sammy is a Mexican-American educator, poet,
spoken word artist, and zine queen. She has found her way back into
poetry after a long hiatus, fully immersing herself in the community
through open mics, workshops, and poetry slams. She writes on topics
such as feminism, racism, working with children, mental health, love,
and heartbreak. Sammy is more often a lover than a fighter but will
tackle heavy topics with grit and grace through poetry and perfor-
mances. You can find samples of her work, upcoming events, shows,
and digital zines on her website prettypetitepoems.com.

Publisher's Note

Daxson publishing was created to help marginalized artists and their allies publish their work, so the world can hear their voice. The vision for this publishing house is to help people get their work out there, and not have them struggle finding their way through the publishing process. Everyone's voice deserves to be heard, and we are here to help. If you are interested in submitting a manuscript, email daxsonpublishing@gmail.com. Support our cause! Buy our books at daxsonpublishing.com.